Developing Prayer Ministry

A New Introduction for Churches

John Leach

Director, Anglican Renewal Ministries

GROVE BOOKS LIMITED
RIDLEY HALL RD CAMBRIDGE CB3 9HU

Contents

1. Introduction 3
2. A Theology of Prayer Ministry 4
3. Assessing Your Model 8
4. Introducing and Integrating 14
5. Principles of Prayer Ministry 18
6. Getting Going: Towards a Strategy 22

The Cover Illustration is by Peter Ashton

Copyright © John Leach 2000

First Impression July 2000
ISSN 1470-8531
ISBN 1 85174 437 1

1
Introduction

How can you tell whether or not a church is a charismatic church? In the early days of British renewal it was easy—you watched to see what songs were sung, and whether or not people put their hands in the air while they sung them. The right kind of worship songs and raised hands indicated beyond doubt that you were in a 'renewed' church.

But nowadays it is nowhere near that easy. In my experience of travelling around the country visiting different churches I have observed a significant shift, so that there is now something different which stands out as the defining factor of churches which espouse renewal spirituality: the offering of some kind of prayer ministry during or after services. Not every church which offers such ministry would want to call itself charismatic, of course, but most churches which would be happy to be so labelled do have some kind of prayer ministry available, at least in theory.

At least in theory. Ah, but there's the rub. In fact, prayer ministry is talked about and offered far more than it actually occurs, and when it does occur it can be less than perfect in several different ways. There may be a great deal of reluctance on the part of anyone in the congregation actually to go forward to receive ministry; it may be tagged on at the end of a service rather than being integrated into it; it may be led unhelpfully from the front or handled ineffectually by those ministering; it may be offered unthinkingly with no real theological basis.

This booklet is an attempt to address the question 'How can we begin to do prayer ministry more effectively?' John Wimber, who was a major catalyst in getting prayer ministry onto the agenda of the British church, taught us that if we are to introduce something new into the life of the church we need three things: a theology; a model; and lots of practice. In other words, we need first to demonstrate that there is a biblical basis for what we are trying to do, then we need an accessible way of actually beginning to do it, and finally we need to keep on doing it until we learn to do it effectively. This book will attempt to provide something of the first two—the third will be up to you!

2
A Theology of Prayer Ministry

We ought to begin by defining exactly what we mean by the term 'prayer ministry,' but it will be easier to do that later rather than sooner, after we have examined the theological premises on which it is based. Once we understand why we should do it, it will be much easier to understand what it is we are doing.

If we limit the concept so that 'prayer ministry' means nothing more than 'healing ministry,' then theological rationales abound.[1] My own pilgrimage has taken me through several different theological models.

In my youth, it was 'If it be thy will.' We believed in theory in God's power directly to affect people's lives, but we had to beware of dictating to the Almighty what he should do, so we ended every prayer with the safety clause 'If it be thy will.' Sadly, it never seemed to be. Then we had the 'Faith' model. We were pointed to verses in the Bible which made extravagant claims for the success of our prayers, and we were told that the problem when real life just did not measure up was a lack of faith. None of this 'If it be thy will'—just name it and claim it. Believe that you already have what you are asking for and it is yours.

Then some healing gurus began to teach that healing always *did* happen, and that if the victim appeared to remain unhealed, it was because they had not yet 'walked out' or 'claimed' their healing. When we pray, God does it, by definition, and we have to go away and live as if it has happened. Then, of course, the 'Praise' model told us to thank God for our illnesses. We have an altogether too negative view of sickness and suffering, and we should come to God in gratitude for our ailments and thank him for his great love and mercy in inflicting them. Several books told stories of dramatic healings after such praise.

But what exactly is healing? Another theological model tells us that we only get healed when we get to heaven. We should be striving for 'wholeness,' not mere 'curing,' the removal of troublesome sicknesses. Inner peace and integration are far more important than being able to walk, hear or see again.[2]

Finally I arrived at what I called the 'Despair' model, which said in a nutshell that if God wanted to heal someone, he would, and that if he did not, he would not, and nothing I could do or say could affect his decision one way or the other, so what was the point? This at last provided a satisfactory model for

---

1   This subject is addressed in a more scholarly way than I have the space or skill to attempt in H H Knight, 'God's Faithfulness and God's Freedom: A comparison of contemporary theologies of healing' *Journal of Pentecostal Theology* 2 (1993) pp 65–89.
2   Personally I thought that 'wholeness' meant being spiritually integrated *and* physically well, but the sort of healing Jesus did is clearly not quite the real thing for aficionados of this model.

4

me, and I lived quite happily not praying for anyone for some years.[3]

The problem with each of these theologies, it seems to me, is that whilst they have all (with the possible exception of the last) grasped a little bit of biblical teaching, they do not provide an overall scheme which is satisfactory. Not least, none of them takes seriously a theology of failure, addressing the fact that it is empirically true that many if not most of the people for whom we pray remain unhealed, faith, praise and so on notwithstanding. So when I discovered the 'kingdom' model of healing I was thrilled to find that whilst it helped me to see people healed, it also helped me when they were not, and helped me to care for those not healed without loading guilt onto them.

The Kingdom of God[4]

I came from a very conservative background to train for the ministry at King's College, London in the halcyon days of the seventies, when a highly critical approach to Scripture ruled academia. In our New Testament lectures we were told that Jesus came to inaugurate the kingdom of God, the rule of God exercised on earth as it is in heaven. Jesus preached about the kingdom, and demonstrated it by bringing God's liberation to those who had become oppressed or enslaved by Satan, through sickness or demonization. Every miracle, whilst it was no doubt good for the person upon whom it was done, had even greater significance—it demonstrated the victory of God, and it meant one small step of advancement for the kingdom and one further defeat for Satan.

The problem was, though, that no-one actually believed any of this. Few of my lecturers believed that Jesus really did heal any sick people or deal with any demons; that was just the mythology which a great teacher inevitably attracted to himself. But if he *had* healed or delivered, that was what it would have meant. Furthermore, I did not believe any of it, not because of any liberal tendencies, but because I already knew that Jesus came to preach a gospel of Pauline justification by faith. I simply did not hear when anyone told me anything different.

But when several years later I first encountered John Wimber, every bell within me began to ring as he expounded exactly the same kingdom theology, and then proceeded to demonstrate it before our very eyes. Since then I have become more and more convinced of the biblical validity of this theological model, as well as its effectiveness in providing a background to prayer ministry.

Others have provided a far more detailed and eloquent account of kingdom theology than I have space to do here,[5] but in outline it concerns the ministry of Jesus to set free those who were under the control of Satan and who were thus

---

3   For further reflections on charismatic theology see T Smail, A Walker and N Wright *Charismatic Renewal: The Search for a Theology* (London: SPCK, 1993, 1995).
4   Apologies to those who know this backwards, but at a recent New Wine seminar about two-thirds of those present (perhaps 400 people) indicated that, although they thought they knew it, hearing it set out again had reminded them of its importance. I hope I might do the same for you in this brief summary.
5   See, for example, G E Ladd, *A Theology of the New Testament* (London: Lutterworth, 1974).

oppressed and victimised by him, and plagued with all sorts of ills of body, mind, spirit, relationships and society. In effect humankind chose at the fall to have Satan rather than God rule over them, and thus became the victims of a cruel and vicious dictator who trapped them in sin and inflicted upon them all sorts of ills. People still believed in something better, but found themselves unable to see very much of it. So they developed a somewhat apocalyptic vision of the future when this present evil age, over which Satan ruled, would be replaced by the age to come. God would break in, undo all the work of Satan, and rescue his people. By the time of Jesus' earthly ministry, this worldview was *de rigeur* in Palestine. The people to whom he came were expecting the imminent coming of the rule or reign of God (that, rather than a piece of geographical territory, is what the words translated 'kingdom' mean in the Bible) and in particular they were expecting this rule to manifest itself in the overthrow of the hated Roman occupying force. So when Jesus burst onto the scene announcing that 'The kingdom of God is at hand' (Mark 1.15) Jewish ears would have pricked up everywhere. But some illusions had to be shattered. The kingdom was a spiritual, not an earthly, political kingdom, and though it was 'at hand,' it was not yet fully in evidence. Oscar Cullman's seminal *Christ and Time*[6] expounds this concept of 'eschatological tension,' the fact that the kingdom is here in part, but not yet fully realized. The New Testament church lived, as we do today, in the 'end times.' The term simply means the gap between the inauguration of the kingdom by Jesus and its final consummation with Jesus' return in glory.

The Kingdom Battle

Part of Jesus' ministry was to call others into the battle, and to endow them with power and authority against Satan. But it was always a case of partial success; they won some and they lost some. Still today the battle goes on: Christians are called to join in the fight and to see the work of Satan to harm and harass people defeated. In particular, we are called to preach good news to people—you do not have to live as you are; you can come out from under the oppressive rule of Satan and come under the just and gentle rule of Jesus. We are called to pray that the inflicted harm done to people directly or indirectly by Satan would be replaced with the blessings of Jesus. But we must also understand that when people follow Jesus they will begin to suffer in a different way, as they place themselves deliberately in the way of persecution by refusing to capitulate with the sin, evil and godlessness of the current regime.

However, we have neither total freedom nor total autonomy in this task. Jesus told his followers that he could only do what he saw his Father doing (John 5.19) and so his ministry consisted in approximately equal proportions of listening to the Father in prayer and obeying what he heard. So our ministry too

---

6   Cullman, O, *Christ and Time* (London: SCM, 1950).

is to be guided by God; we cannot go in and empty a hospital any more than Jesus emptied the porticoes of the Pool of Bethesda (in fact he was directed to one person only; John 5.5–6). Prayer ministry is more like driving a tram than a car; we need to stay on the rails of God's revealed will, not steer where we like.

Praying the Kingdom

Thus prayer ministry (at last we can attempt to define it) is the bringing of the kingdom of God into lives which have in some way been harmed, attacked or even shattered by the direct or indirect work of the Devil. Healing of mind or body is one small part of it, but it is much wider; where any part of our being or relationships has become damaged or is at dis-ease, we pray for God's inbreaking power to make a difference. Each step forward is another small step in the continuing advance of the kingdom of God, another small area in which his will, and not that of Satan, is being done.

But what I really appreciate about kingdom theology is that it provides a model which does justice to our frequent failure in the healing ministry.[7] It takes eschatological tension seriously. If the kingdom had not yet arrived, we could only pray into the future with hope. If it had arrived in full consummation, we could pray in the present with certainty. But because we live in the gap between arrival and consummation we will know both success and failure, power and powerlessness, and of course *some* power, and *partial* success. Prayer ministry is a battle, and there are all sorts of reasons on a purely human level why soldiers lose battles. It also takes seriously the frustrating fact that God chooses to work through and with fallen humans, rather than just zapping people himself.

Obviously acceptance of this theological model will have a profound effect on the way we talk about prayer ministry in the church. We have to walk a few tightropes. We never make extravagant promises which we do not have the power to keep, and yet we seek to build faith rather than destroy it. Somewhere between 'Come forward now and you'll be healed!' and 'You can ask for prayer if you like, but the chances are not a lot is going to make much difference to you' lies a more helpful form of words which builds confidence in God but takes the battle seriously. Similarly there is a tightrope between celebrating an all-powerful God and acknowledging human weakness, and between God's general desire for the wholeness and *shalom* of all people and his specific sovereign choice to act or not to act in any given individual situation. Running a ministry time is not an easy task with so many creative ways to get it wrong!

---

[7] By 'failure' I mean not seeing the specific healing for which we are asking. God will almost always bless people in some way, so prayer is never a total failure, but I personally refuse to play word-games about 'curing' and healing. If I have asked for a God to get someone out of a wheelchair and he does not, that looks pretty much like failure to me, and the honest thing to do is to face it!

3
Assessing Your Model

Having articulated a theology for prayer ministry, we now turn to our model. Whilst it is vital that we get our theology right and in agreement with Scripture, when it comes to models we can be much more flexible. As long as our ministry accurately reflects good biblical theology, we may actually choose to do it in a variety of ways. Whether we go for a 'Vineyard' style, a 'Pentecostal' model, a 'Sacramental' approach or any of a variety of other ways of conducting ministry is really up to an individual church. Having said that, there are some questions we need to ask of our chosen model to ensure that it is both helpful and biblical.

It is not the intention of this book to explain or promote one particular way of doing prayer ministry, but I do want to suggest some criteria against which any model may be assessed. You may be thinking of introducing prayer ministry into the life of your church, and you may have seen various ways of doing it in action in other churches. Alternatively you may already be including ministry, but feeling the need for some kind of an overhaul. In either case, the following questions will be good ones to ask of your current or prospective model. They should help you to identify strengths and weaknesses—there may even be a realization that the way we are currently doing things gives messages with which we do not actually agree.

Why Models?

It sounds very spiritual when Christians say 'I am not a Baptist, nor an Anglican, nor a Roman Catholic; I am just a Christian' but in fact it is naïve, because given the nature of the church at the moment we inevitably have to belong somewhere and thus bear a label of some sort. In the same way those who claim not to be interested in models or methods but only in healing the sick may sound wonderfully impressive, but the fact is that when they pray for people they do it in a particular way. So how might we choose which model will become the one for our church? What factors will affect this choice?

i) The Leader's Personality

Like it or not, the personal preferences of a church leader, vicar or minister cannot help but affect the life of the church in all sorts of ways. A quiet unassuming leader will probably be uncomfortable with a big, up-front style based around a gifted 'healer,' whilst a more extravert leader may find a 'listening' approach just a little bit boring.

ii) The Church's Personality

In a similar way churches have personalities, which may or may not be closely aligned with that of their leaders. This personality is often expressed in terms of 'values,' the things which are important to us as a church. If our greatest value is peace, quiet and dignity there will be some models which we will not be at all comfortable with! If we are driven as a church by the need for evangelism, we may find that most of our prayer ministry takes place not in church at all, but in the homes, shops and offices where the congregation live, move and have their being. Any model must be applicable to non-church settings as well as helpful during services. There may not, after all, be an altar rail in Asda.

Under this heading come liturgical constraints which our particular church ethos dictates and which we value; these too will affect the model we choose.

iii) Our Influences

As well as questions of personality, we need to recognize that we are likely to adopt models based on those who have been the first or the strongest influence on us. John Wimber's model for prayer ministry has had such a profound effect on the British church, and in particular on the Anglican church, simply because he was the first to bring a clearly articulated and accessible model which resonated with many of the Anglican values like shared ministry, dignity and thoughtfulness.

There may be other influences too, and I set these out not in any way to make value judgments but simply to help us be alert to the fact that these very human factors will affect our selection of a model for ministry. But we are not at the mercy of these influences; we do have a choice in how we do it.

So what criteria might we use in deciding which model we will major on? I will suggest six questions which I think it is important for us to answer.

What is the Source of Power?

When we pray for people expecting that some subjective or objective change will occur, it follows that the power for that change must come from somewhere. It is important to ask of any model 'What is the power-source?' There are at least four possibilities:

i) God's 'Natural' Power

God has built into the universe natural healing properties. If I get some kind of an infection, my body will usually deal with the problem by itself, although in severe cases it may need help from the natural products which God has helped scientists to discover and put to use. If this is our power-source, prayer becomes more of an affirmation than a request, and it may be focussed more on the inner state of the victim than on God's power to intervene and make a difference.

ii) God's 'Supernatural' Power

Some models see God as much more invasive than this, and the prayer is a specific request to him to do something which will bring about objective change in the state of the victim. Something may well happen naturally in the long-term, but that is not good enough; we pray for, and expect, God to make a difference, a difference which would not have been made had we not prayed.

iii) Human Power

Some models major on the power which God has put naturally into the human spirit to work towards wholeness. The 'power of positive thinking,' human potential counselling, the belief that the solution to many of one's problems lies within—all these are manifestations of a belief in human power, and some models of ministry owe a lot to it.

Most Christians probably do not have a problem with these models, even if we want to move beyond some of them. They do clearly reflect some truth; there are natural healing processes built into the human body and spirit, and God often does want us to receive his strength and courage to face our difficulties. But a fourth possibility is less acceptable, though no less real.

iv) Demonic Power

Christians would perceive that some models of ministry get their power directly from the other side, and would therefore want to shun particular practices. In my experience there is real genuine spiritual power out there, which can do some good to people. Jesus was even accused of using demonic power in his deliverance ministry (Matt 12.24). But it only does good superficially, and there is always a pay-off at a deeper level. It is common for a genuine physical healing to be followed by spiritual or mental distress or breakdown. We would rightly want to shun any model ultimately which did people harm.

So if prayer ministry requires power, from where, according to your favourite model, does it come? It goes without saying that only power directly or indirectly from the God and Father of our Lord Jesus Christ is worth having in the church.

What is the Role of the 'Minister'?

When we pray for someone, who is actually doing the work? And just who is allowed to do the praying? Am I healing someone, or is God? The Bible is ambivalent about this. Peter is very clear when addressing Aeneas that 'Jesus Christ heals you' (Acts 9.34), but the disciples are sent out by Jesus to heal the sick themselves (Mt 10.8 and parallels). This may be splitting hairs, but it might become significant if your model has a high value on a charismatic 'healer' who may give the impression that it is he or she who does it all. Surely the old illustration of Moses at the Red Sea is relevant here. The miracle required two things: Moses' stick and God's power. When Moses stretched out his stick, God sent his power, and the Sea parted. God and Moses worked in co-operation; without God's power the miracle could not have happened, and without Moses' stick the miracle would not have happened. Healing and ministry is surely of this nature—the power comes from God, but what we do releases it.

So who does the 'ministry'? The duly ordained minister alone? The charismatic 'healer' in front of whom those desiring prayer queue up? The whole of the body of Christ in that place? If so how is that organized? Or do the recipients pray themselves, with the 'ministers' in the role of spiritual midwives? Is it those with badges and therefore presumably some training and expertise in ministry who pray? Or those who have the 'gift of healing'? If so, what is your theology of 'having' spiritual gifts?

This is an important question to ask, since it is possible to have adopted a model for all sorts of reasons (sometimes stretching back into history) without ever having considered what that model is teaching about the nature of ministry. Can you only do it if you have been ordained? Is it meant to be a free-for-all? Do you really agree with what your model is actually saying?

The Dignity of the Victim

How does your model treat those who are on the receiving end? And how does that measure up to the way we would imagine Jesus treating the needy people with whom he came into contact? Is someone seeking prayer seen as just the next person in a queue, or are people treated as individuals, special and unique? Is time available, or are they made to feel part of a production line or sausage machine? Is it right to use people as public spectacles to encourage faith and/or enhance the 'healer's' reputation? Sometimes 'words of knowledge' are used to expose publicly the needs of individuals. How is this handled in your model? And do people feel blamed if the desired outcome of the prayer is not apparently forthcoming? Whatever else we may do to people, we surely need to treat them with love, respect and honour, and we need to beware of models which devalue, expose or exploit people.

What is the Place of Suffering?

Prayer ministry must take suffering seriously, not least because many of the people who seek ministry do so from places of suffering. But again different models do in fact say things about it which we may or may not believe theologically. One school of thought would see all suffering as bad, evil and to be resisted. God wants you fit, healthy and wealthy, not in a general sense but specifically here and now. Prayer ministry is there to remove all nastiness from your life so that you can live in victory and wholeness. Another model would see suffering as a sign of God's displeasure, or perhaps as a punishment for specific sins.[8] Still another would major on the redemptive power of suffering: it is good for you, and is therefore to be endured with patience. And a popular view, as we have mentioned, told us some years ago that we should be thankful for our problems and weaknesses.

So we need to ask what our model teaches or implies about suffering, and whether we really agree.

What Are Our Expectations of Healing?

We have already noted the existence of a school of thought which distinguishes between 'healing' and mere 'curing.' So for what exactly are we praying? The liturgical words of the *Alternative Service Book* seem to capture this dilemma beautifully: 'Comfort and heal all those who suffer…give them courage and hope in their troubles.'[9] Which is it? Are we asking God to heal them, or to help them to feel better about being ill?

One factor in thinking through this issue must surely have to do with what Jesus did in his healing ministry, and the way the early church followed in his footsteps. I have simply been unable to find one example of Jesus helping someone to cope better with a disability. He tended, as far as the text tells us, to go for the big problems, like blindness, lameness, deafness and even deadness—and reverse the situation. The apostles similarly set their sights high, although there is that bewildering passage where the somewhat unhealthy Timothy is encouraged to look after his stomach better with the occasional nip of wine (1 Tim 5.23). Clearly full and perfect wholeness is only available to us on the other side of death or Jesus' return, but the question of how much it is right to expect now is still open. Just what did Jesus mean when he promised that we would be able to do even greater works than he had done (John 14.12)? I recently read somewhere that the one thing he cannot have meant is that we would do lesser works than he did! What size expectations does your model have, and do they match up to Bible-sized ones?

What is the Understanding of Failure?

Again, we have mentioned this with respect to a theology of ministry—what of our models? If someone does not receive from God that for which they were hoping, how are things left? Four possibilities present themselves:

i) It is Your Fault!

It might be unconfessed sin, it might be lack of faith, or any number of other factors, but victims are left with no doubt that there is something wrong with

---

8   For an examination of the relationship between sin and sickness from a Pentecostal point of view, see J C Thomas, 'The Devil, Disease and Deliverance' *Journal of Pentecostal Theology* 2 (1993) pp 25–50 and the monograph with the same title (Sheffield: Sheffield Academic Press, JPTS 13, 1998).
9   From the intercession section of the *ASB* Rite A Communion service, p 125.

them, in addition to the wrong thing they came to seek prayer about. This may well be true, of course. Someone refusing, for example, to deal with an issue of forgiveness or repentance which God has revealed should certainly not expect to find fresh grace from God if he or she has refused the grace to deal with the key issue. But whether we blame all failure on the victim as a matter of policy is another matter entirely.

ii) It is God's Fault!

Sometimes the model implies that failure is due to some lack of will on the part of God. Few question his *ability* to heal, but his *will* to heal in any given situation cannot be taken as a matter of quite so much certainty. Sometimes this is linked with the explanation above: it is God's will to act, but just not for you!

iii) It is My Fault!

As the one doing the praying, it might be my fault if the desired outcome was not achieved. If we take seriously the soldiers-in-a-battle model which we have mentioned, it is quite likely to be my fault. Does our model expect us to own up and face this, and what does that do to us if we do admit it? And do the recipients feel able to ask for more prayer on a future occasion, or was that it? Are they now stuck for ever?

iv) It is No-one's Fault!

It may be no-one's fault because healing *has* in fact happened. Nothing may *appear* to have happened, but give it time, perhaps act as though it had happened, and the visible results will follow. Clearly not all answers to prayer will be instantaneous, or instantaneously recognizable, any more than they were for Jesus. On the other hand, it might really be the case that nothing has happened! What does your chosen model imply? And how does it help you with thinking about further prayer or ongoing pastoral support?

These questions, then, should be ruthlessly applied to a possible or existing model of ministry within your church, in order to make sure that what we are doing says what we want to be saying. In other words, our practice should be the visible outworking of our theology and our values: if there is any mismatch between the two, we need to adjust either one or the other.

4
Introducing and Integrating

So we have considered our theology and our methodology for prayer ministry. We may be starting from scratch, or we may be giving the system an overhaul, but we still need to answer the question 'Where, how and when do we actually do this?' In this section I want to turn to a detailed examination of how prayer ministry fits within the life and worship of a local church.

Let me begin from the end, and say that our aim in offering prayer ministry must surely be that on one level it is no big deal. Praying for one another and seeing the power of God's kingdom released ought surely to be just something Christians do when they get together. We do not make a big fuss about some of the other things we do. When we meet we read the Bible and sing songs of worship. No-one, I notice, has written a Grove booklet about how to fit singing into your Sunday services—we just do it, and to all intents and purposes we have always just done it. Prayer ministry is only an issue, I believe, because it is something which has been lost from the life of the church, so having rediscovered it, we struggle somewhat to know quite what to do with it.

It is not quite as simple as singing songs, of course, because we can do that quite adequately without God being involved at all, whereas prayer ministry is all about the involvement of God. This gives an element of unpredictability about the whole thing which makes it slightly more difficult to plan for, but I still believe it ought to be a natural part of what Christians do when we meet.

Of course the gifts of the Holy Spirit were not just given for use in the church. David Pytches' famous dictum that 'the meeting place is the learning place for the market place' is exactly right. Prayer ministry ought to happen naturally not just when Christians meet with other Christians, but also when they meet with other people. We have already noted the need for a model which can be done just as successfully between the pasta and the tinned tomatoes in Tesco as it can during a church service, but I believe the more we see it as natural to pray in church, the more readily and easily we will be able to pray elsewhere.

So we are aiming for prayer ministry to be naturally integrated into public worship. But immediately we hit some constraints. It is not as simple as saying 'just do it'; there are some factors to take into consideration. I have identified seven of them, but there are surely others.

1) Time

Prayer ministry, if it is to be done at any depth at all, takes time, and may take lots of time. Different factors will decide how much of it we have available, and how much of that we want to give to ministry. A Sunday evening service, for example, is usually less pressurized than a Sunday morning. Fewer children will be present, the dinner is not in the oven, and people may regard themselves as being out for the evening, rather than for an hour or two as in the morning. It is less likely that there will be visitors in the typical church, so if the service is still going strong at 11.30pm, it is to be regarded as a success. A morning service which was still going on five hours later might well be regarded as a disaster!

There are two schools of thought in the church about this. One says that we should not quench the Spirit, and that if God is still at work we should go with it and not get uptight about time. The other says that in the long term people, and especially visitors, will simply stop coming if they know that they will be in for a marathon, and so in the interests of the longer view we should regulate time more carefully. Personally I am a subscriber to the latter view: I used to time our morning services ruthlessly, and at closing time I would instantly chop whatever was going on. If people wanted to stay behind for more ministry that was fine, but the congregation as a whole knew with certainty when they would be able to escape at the latest by 11.00am, and probably earlier. This trust was never abused, but they also knew that the evening services would be free from this kind of constraint, and might well go on longer, although we would still have an official finish when we set people free to leave or to stay.

So if we have a limited amount of time available, we need then to apportion it between the different ingredients in the service, of which prayer ministry is only one. It is this, I believe, which leads many churches to do their ministry after the service has officially ended, and there is logic in this, except that it cannot help but give the message that ministry is an optional extra for those who like that sort of thing, and that it is not as central or important as reading the Bible, listening to a sermon or singing hymns—a message which we might not actually wish to give.

2) Space

Tied in with this are the physical constraints of the space we have to work with. Some churches have a multitude of side-chapels which can be used for ministry. This can help with the time constraint by allowing ministry to be going on at the same time as something else, for example the administration of communion. But if you are meeting in a school gym or church hall that might be more difficult. And again, what does it say about its importance if ministry is only ever done off behind a screen somewhere, to all intents and purposes in a separate room?

3) Openness

By this I mean the degree to which the congregation are happy with prayer ministry being a part of what they do as a church. A New Church congregation may well be totally at ease with the most outrageous things happening during worship (at least that is my Anglican fantasy about New Churches). People probably joined the church exactly because such things were on the agenda. A typical Anglican church will have a variety of different congregations which will have been affected to varying degrees by renewal, ranging from 'not in the slightest' to 'a bit.' The way ministry is handled (if at all) during different Sunday services may vary tremendously.

The time constraints are linked with this to some degree. An early morning communion service may have very little flexibility in terms of timing: it has taken somewhere between thirty-eight and forty-one minutes every week for the last sixty years, and no-one expects anything different. Besides, the main Sunday service starts at 9.30am, and by 9am the musicians are tuning up, the coffee-makers are setting out their wares, and so on. But those who choose to come to the sort of evening service where there is freedom for the Spirit to move generally have chosen to be there exactly because there is freedom for the Spirit to move.

4) Vision

The way we introduce prayer ministry will to some degree be controlled by where we see it going in the longer term. It might be my aim, as an Anglican priest, to do ministry in a kind of 'Vineyard' style, standing the congregation up, inviting the Spirit to come, and seeing who falls over first. Or I might have no more dramatic expectations than that people will kneel quietly at the communion rail and meet with God in the peace and quiet. Either of these might be entirely appropriate, but knowing where we are headed will affect how we start out. Often our long-term aims remain unarticulated, but to see clearly a vision of where we would like to be can help us to build a strategy for getting there.

5) Liturgy

All churches are, of course, liturgical; the difference is that some use liturgy deliberately and proudly, whilst others use it in an unwritten but equally regular way. But a further constraint arises if the church services are liturgical in the sense of being driven by a book. This touches on the time and space questions, but takes them further—do we expect the Spirit to move in spite of the set liturgy, in between the liturgy, or in and through it?

6) Personnel

Another limiting factor, which will again tie in with time and space, but also with questions of openness and vision, has to do with just who is doing the praying. If only the 'priest' is allowed to minister, the prayer may be brought back into more central focus spatially, but will consume more time than if a team of people minister. If the ministry is something of a free-for-all (for example praying in small clusters throughout the congregation) it may happen relatively quickly, but will require a high degree of openness. It will, though, be less demanding architecturally.

7) User-friendliness
Finally there is the question of what our handling of ministry will say to those unused to it, and in particular visitors, of which Anglican churches in particular may receive many who have come to have a child in the extended family baptized, or to hear their Banns of Marriage, or to follow up a family funeral. Personally I am convinced that whilst things like a warm welcome, good music, relevant preaching, and even ample car parking, are vitally important, the single biggest factor to draw people to church is a felt sense of the presence of God. They might find it a bit scary, but they are more likely to come back for more than if the service was predictable but to all intents and purposes Godless. Of course, immediate exposure on someone's first visit to congregation-wide ministry in groups of three for a Toronto anointing may just be taking things a bit too far too quickly. But I am sure that it is right that we avoid making ministry all so secretive that no visitor even notices that we do ever pray for one another and that God often answers such prayer.

So all these constraints, and no doubt several more, all woven together and interconnected, will affect how we might go about introducing prayer ministry. Before I suggest a possible strategy for beginning prayer ministry, I want to draw out some general principles which I think arise from the theology of prayer ministry as well as from my pastoral experience. Perhaps these principles might be used as a stimulus to further discussion in your local situation.

5
Principles of Prayer Ministry

God wants us to pray for one another. I need not labour this; the New Testament implies or says it directly on every page. This does not need exclusively to be prayer ministry, up close and personal, and clearly includes prayer for others at a distance, but it seems clear that part of the practice of the biblical church was personal prayer with laying on of hands.[10]

It Should Be a Natural Part of What We Do

Prayer for others should come naturally to Christians, not least in order that it becomes natural for them to offer it to non-Christians. It is not something weird, to be done behind closed doors, nor something so special that we have to work ourselves up to it or only do it once a month on a Wednesday evening. John Wimber was once asked how he prepared for ministry. He answered, epitomizing his 'naturally supernatural' approach, 'I finish my diet Coke and turn off the TV.'

We Should Seek to Draw People In, Not Drive Them Out

If it is our perception that some people in the church are not as open as we should perhaps like them to be to the practice of prayer ministry, and are therefore missing out on possible grace and spiritual growth, our aim as church leaders should be to draw them in deeper to something which we believe will do them good. But we are unlikely to do that if we drop them in at the deep end, for example by having a Wimber-style 'clinic' at the 8 am Communion Service. That may be our long-term vision, but we need to approach it gently, and find ways of giving people a taste for more of the Spirit without shocking them and putting them off.

In the parish of which I was vicar we had a Wednesday morning Communion which was not known for its charismatic excesses. One week, back in the days of the *ASB* lectionary,[11] I was preparing for the service. It was the week of the Eighth Sunday before Easter, so the theme was 'Christ the Healer.' We had done this particular theme every year, but this time I felt that it would be good actually to offer prayer for healing. I explained, from the readings, what I intended to do, and invited any who wanted to receive prayer to remain at the rail after I had given them the wine, and I would do a third sweep and pray for any

---

10　Leaving aside the healing ministry of Jesus, there are references to this kind of prayer in Acts 6.6, 8.17f, 9.12, 9.17, 13.3, 19.6, 28.8, 1 Tim 4.14, 5.22, 2 Tim 1.6, and Heb 6.2 (where it is described as being a part of basic, foundational Christian practice).
11　The series of set themes and readings for the C of E, now superseded by the *Revised Common Lectionary*.

who were still kneeling there, with a short liturgical prayer, and without asking them for details. They could seek prayer for themselves or for others. I was slightly surprised to see a significant uptake of my offer, but even more surprised to see that when I used my short, set liturgical prayer, on some of the most unlikely people, I saw exactly the same signs of the Spirit resting on them that I was used to from 'proper' ministry sessions. We had fluttering eyelids, shaking hands, tears, and even one lady who, had I not gripped her shoulder securely, would have fallen to the floor under the rail. In the porch after the service the general consensus was 'That was lovely. Could we do it again please?' After that, not wanting to go too far too quickly, I instituted prayer ministry in that style at that service on a monthly basis.

Surely it is the case that some people are put off not by the prayer itself, and the encounter with God which it often brings, but by the package in which we wrap it up. Many people at that service came to have a powerful encounter with God, but there was not a single charismatic worship song, no semi-audible muttering in tongues, no words of knowledge, and no forty-five minute sermon. Meeting people where they are, and setting up a ministry style appropriate to the setting, can provide an important way in for people, even if our preferred style and long-term vision is for ministry which is a little more overt. And allowing people to come up on behalf of others can be gloriously releasing for those trained into never showing any weakness publicly.[12]

We Should Play the System, Not Fight It

Those of us from the historic denominations who have been led into prayer ministry by those from newer churches, most notably and most commonly the Vineyard, often seek to dismantle our heritage and style and increasingly take on a 'lowest common denominator' approach to worship and church life, feeling that 'proper church' is a hindrance to the moving of God's Spirit. It is my conviction that nothing could be further from the truth. So often we alienate those who do have a large investment in the system (often the more elderly) by telling them, in effect, that we are going to do away with something they love in order that we can have instead something they are afraid of! No wonder they are less than keen. Surely our aim should be to make ministry accessible to as many people as possible, and we can do that by playing the system. Many Anglicans would rather die than 'come down to the front to receive ministry,' but they are perfectly happy to move to the communion rail during the service, so, as in my Wednesday Communion, let us pray for them there. Anointing with oil may, in some churches, be far more acceptable than laying on hands in small groups, so why not use it? People may prefer the privacy of a side chapel for

---

12 Personally I find the practice of receiving 'proxy' laying on of hands for someone else questionable and unbiblical, but I do think that agreeing in prayer is helpful, so I would often hold the person's hand while we prayed rather than laying hands on their head.

their early experiences of receiving ministry. We may not want to leave them there, but surely we can start them there if it helps build security and confidence. These 'churchy' things need not get in the way of the Spirit; indeed there are increasing signs of newer churches turning to some of the things which have formed the bedrock of the established denominations because they have glimpsed the spiritual power which they can mediate.

Liturgy Should Do What It Says
This deserves a book all to itself, but it is a plea, flowing out from what I have said above, to allow the Spirit to flow through the liturgy and not between it or in spite of it. Why do we need long, extempore prayers invoking the Spirit when the book does it much more simply for us: 'The Lord is here! His Spirit is with us!' Congregations can be helped to let the words do their work if they are told that that is what should happen, and if we slow down and allow time for it to happen. With copious quantities of highly renewal-friendly texts in *Common Worship* and *Patterns for Worship*, we really can play this system too, again giving security and a point of contact for those who actually enjoy the liturgy.

We Should Involve Others, Without Creating an Elite
There may be times when reluctant people will be helped to experience ministry if they have the security of a 'priest' alone ministering, but long-term it will be helpful to train a team. This can save time, allow more personal and in-depth prayer when appropriate, and demystify the ministry. And of course it can allow significantly more divine encounters in Sainsbury's, since they are not all directly dependent on the minister!

Beware the feeling though that you have to be somehow special to be allowed to minister, or that the team is a closed group which no mere mortals can ever penetrate. Badges may be essential in large, more anonymous churches where ministry tends to happen among the congregation, but they are probably superfluous for average-sized churches. Training should be thorough, and there are plenty of opportunities on offer, but try to generate an 'ever-widening' approach to prayer ministry rather than a once-and-for-all trained, badged group whose sole preserve it is to pray.

We Should Expect Great Things, and Explain Everything
People may seek prayer ministry for a variety of reasons: healing, whether physical or emotional; commissioning for some new phase or area of responsibility in the church or in their secular work; refreshing or refilling with the Holy Spirit; the release of new gifts, or an initial baptism in the Spirit; guidance over some important crossroads in life; in response to the preaching or reading of the word—the list goes on. It is my conviction that the point of praying is to see God do something; personally I do not want people more peaceful, I want them

more healed! Surely the Bible, if it shows anything at all about God, shows him as a God who acts. I believe there is a constant spiritual battle going on to erode our faith and hopefulness, and we need to encourage one another on to biblically-sized expectations.

And when God does move, and even when he does not, we need to explain, for the sake of visitors as well as uncertain members of the congregation, what is going on. I became quite adept over the years, in the middle of some of the most outrageous behaviour, confidently saying to the congregation 'Don't worry, that's just people being touched by God. We are quite used to that here!' It was not always strictly one hundred per cent true, but it was very reassuring for visitors.

So we have explored some theology, some thoughts towards a model, and some principles which ought to govern the way we handle ministry. Now for the practice. That is up to you, but I would just give one word of encouragement: start. Then you can fine-tune it along the way.

6
Getting Going: Towards a Strategy

But how do we start? I offer here a possible draft strategy by which prayer ministry might begin to be integrated into the life of a traditional church. Not everything I suggest will work in every situation, of course, but if I were starting from scratch again I might begin by trying a carefully planned strategy along these lines.

Teach Naturally on a God Who Does Things

Whenever the theme or text allows it, preach about a God who is alive, active, and might actually do things among us as we worship. This drip-feeding will help the truth seem natural after a while, and may even make some people begin to ask 'What is he doing among us now?'

Expect Your Preaching to Demand a Response

Another Grove booklet discusses this more fully, and it can helpfully be read as a companion to this one.[13] I doubt if I would actually ask for much public response at this stage in the strategy if the congregation were not comfortable with it, but I would begin by making sure my sermons did not just give information but did involve some expectation that we ought to do something or be something different as a result of having heard it, and that we have a choice over whether to respond or not.

Begin with 'Meditations'

At the end of a sermon you might lead the people in a brief meditation or prayer which makes the response more clear. Make sure it is grace-based, and use biblical imagery when you can. The most reluctant of congregations will have no problem with this approach, in my experience, and you may even like to introduce the idea that if God has spoken to them they might like to seek personal prayer after the service. You will be very lucky if anyone does, but again it drip-feeds the idea in a non-threatening way.

Find an Excuse for Public Response

It might be a special guest service, a healing service, or some other event, but when you feel the time is right, provide an invitation and a gentle way of making a specific response. Again, *Responding to Preaching* will give you some ideas about how to do this.

---

13   John Leach, *Responding to Preaching* (Grove Worship booklet W 139)

GETTING GOING: TOWARDS A STRATEGY

Make it Culturally Appropriate

If you think you can get away with inviting people forward for personal prayer ministry from scratch, go for it, but it is more likely that a different approach will be preferable earlier on. The use of symbolic action is often helpful. Inviting people to light a small candle as a symbol of whatever and placing it silently before a cross usually works well, as does placing a stone on the Table, picking up a seed, or anything else which is not too contrived. Quite apart from the power of the symbolism (which you should not underestimate), this action reinforces the fact that God asks us to respond to him, and it gets people off their bottoms and down to the front, an essential precursor to more deliberate prayer ministry.

Expose Some Keenies to Your Model

Some of your sheep will hear the voice of God in your voice as you lead the church gently towards ministry, and will become keen to see more. It can be helpful to take them to events where ministry of the style you are working towards happens naturally. This will mean that at least a few people know where you are headed, and will welcome the progress you are making.

Train Some Ministry Team People

Unless the model you are going for demands that you do it all, you will need to begin to have some others who can be trusted by you and the congregation to pray and minister. All sorts of resources are available, so I will not dwell on this here.[14] But do try to avoid the 'elite' feel we mentioned earlier.

Begin to Offer Prayer Occasionally But Regularly

You will need to judge how you do this in the light of the constraints mentioned above, but it is important sooner or later that you do begin.

Discuss it When People Have Seen it, Not Before

You will probably want to get the agreement of the PCC or whatever sooner or later, but in my experience it is better to discuss something they have already seen in action. This will mean that the discussion is based on objective observation rather than subjective fantasy and horror stories from elsewhere. If you have been doing your job properly up till now, people will realize that it is not too bad really!

---

14 Personally I have found no better methodology than that originating from the teaching of John Wimber and now taught by David Pytches and others involved in New Wine. Key books are John Wimber, *Power Evangelism* and *Power Healing* (London: Hodder and Stoughton, 1985/86), David Pytches, *Come Holy Spirit* (London: Hodder and Stoughton, 1985) and Peter Lawrence, *Signs and Blunders* (Crowborough: Monarch, 1994).

DEVELOPING PRAYER MINISTRY

Share Stories, But Not About Manifestations

As ministry becomes more and more commonplace, well-chosen testimonies will encourage people to join in. But do not fall into the trap common in some circles of majoring on the outrageous manifestations of the Spirit, how quickly I hit the ground, how dramatically I twitched and how many times I vomited before the demon left. Stick to stories of how good Jesus is and what a difference he has made, and you will not go far wrong.

Offer one-to-one prayer in pastoral situations...

...and encourage others to do the same. This again will raise the profile of prayer ministry: if people have met God as you prayed with them at home during a visit, they will feel more comfortable in receiving prayer in church.

Be Seen to Receive Ministry Yourself

This does two things. It shows that you are just as much in need of prayer as anyone else, and it models openness and lack of fear. If people never see you on the receiving end, they will begin to feel that you are trying to push them somewhere you are unwilling to go yourself.

All this strategy may take years to get through, but you will build a firm foundation if you take the time to do it carefully and gently. The alternative approach, however, is to invite a visiting preacher for the weekend to do it all for you in one fell swoop!

But however you get there, once prayer ministry is recognized as a part of what you do, keep doing it. All sorts of factors and forces will be around to erode what you have carefully built. Make sure that what you have worked and prayed into being you do not lose through neglect. Keeping prayer ministry on the agenda can be every bit as hard as getting it on in the first place.

So now, in the immortal words of John Wimber, 'Go and do the stuff!'